Goodnight Dog
in the Duck Pond

ISBN: 1461108551
ISBN-13: 978-1461108559

Library of Congress Control Number: 2011906234
CreateSpace, North Charleston, SC

Goodnight Dog
in the Duck Pond

story by Jane Bash
art by nemo

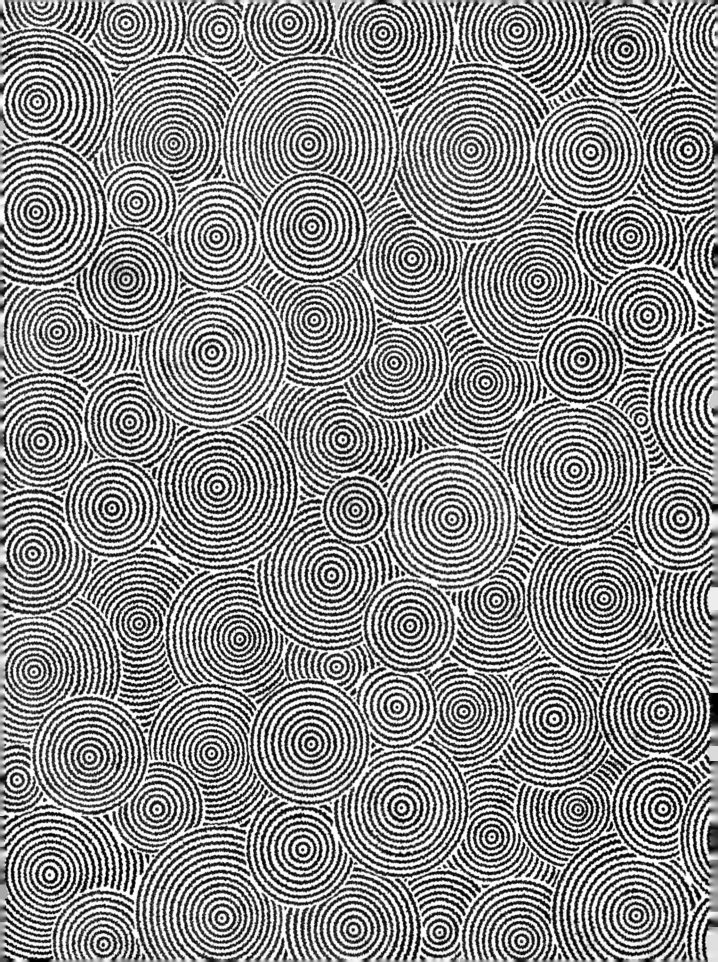

Dedicated to the animals,
and to the people who
appreciate our projects.

Mr. Patrick told Shawn to put
all the animals to bed for the night.

He chose to watch the late, late, very late night movie instead.

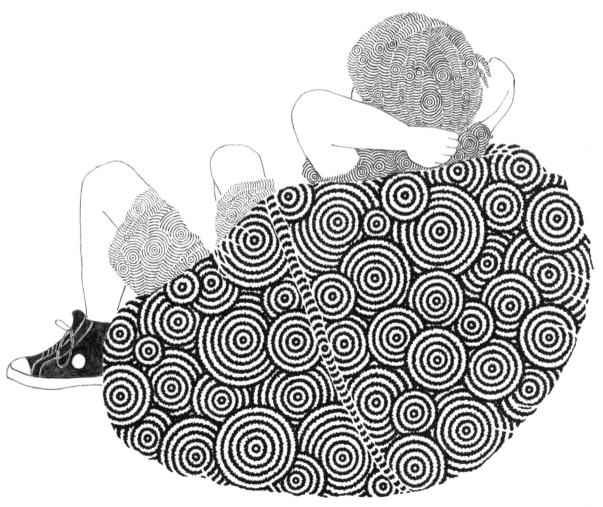

Shawn forgot what his father asked.
He turned off the TV and went to bed.

Just as his head rested on the fluffy pillow,
he remembered all the animals.

"Oh, no! I forgot to put the animals to bed!"

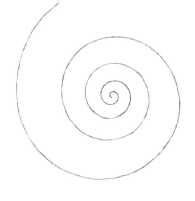

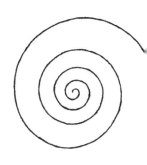

Shawn descended the stairs.
He felt very, very, very, sleepy.

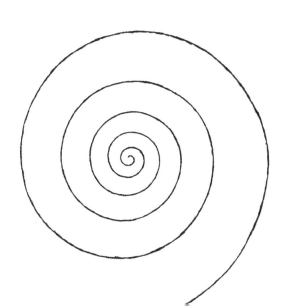

He took the *chicken*
to the *doghouse*,

and the *cow* to
the chicken coop.

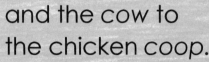

He moved the *goat*
to the cow *barn*,

and the *pig* to
the goat *pen*.

He placed the *rabbit* in the pig *sty*,

and led the *horse* to the rabbit *hutch*.

He brought the *duck* to the horse *stable*,

and finally, finally, finally, he put the *dog* in the duck *pond* for the night.

STY

HUTCH

STABLE

POND

8

9

Silly boy! Shawn stumbled back to the house, ascended the stairs, and fell into his human bed with his clothes still on. He was asleep immediately.

11

12

The animals did not know what was happening.
These were not the right beds for tonight,
or any night!

Dog would not stand for this.
"No! No! Absolutely, no!" Dog barked.
She took charge sorting out all the bed problems.

PEN

"*Pig!* Out of the goat pen and into your *sty!*

STY

Rabbit! Out of the pig sty and into your *hutch!*"

HUTCH

17

"Cow! Out of the chicken coop and into your *barn!*

Goat! Out of the cow barn and into your *pen!*"

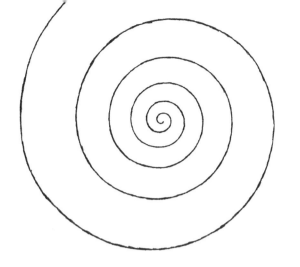

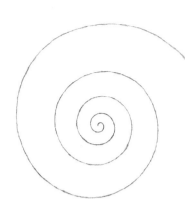

"*Chicken!* Out of my doghouse and into your *coop!*"

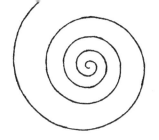

"Now I can finally, finally, finally
go to bed in my *doghouse*!"

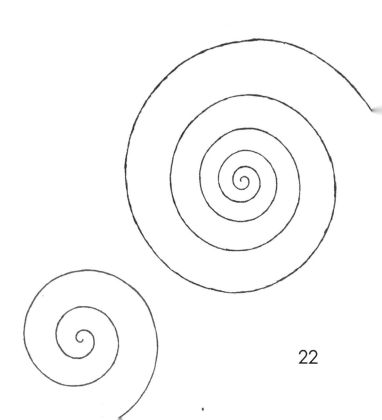

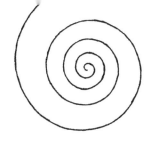

After the chaos and commotion,
Dog curled up in bed and barked,
"Good night!"

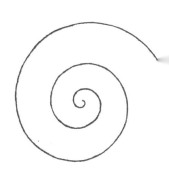

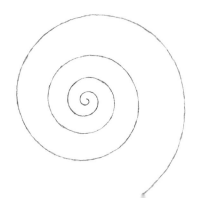

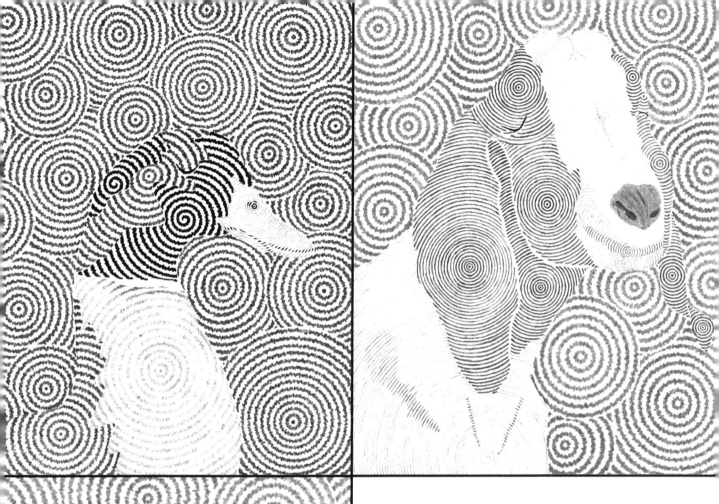

"Sleep tight!" answered all the animals that were tucked into their very own beds.

THE END

Author Bio

Jane Bash earned a Master's Degree in Education and taught for over fifteen years. Her award winning stories and educational musicals have delighted students and children in both the United States and Mexico. This animated bedtime story was inspired by Jane's favorite ranch dog, Buck.

Artist Bio

Nemo and his design partner Hannah Dreiss rose to international acclaim from a design and architectural background. Nemo's unique swirl and spiral designs are licensed with manufacturing companies and their work is represented in several galleries across the United States. Collectors from multiple countries across the globe have invested in their original works.

CPSIA information can be obtained
at www.ICGtesting.com
Printed in the USA
LVIW022137290812

296615LV00005B